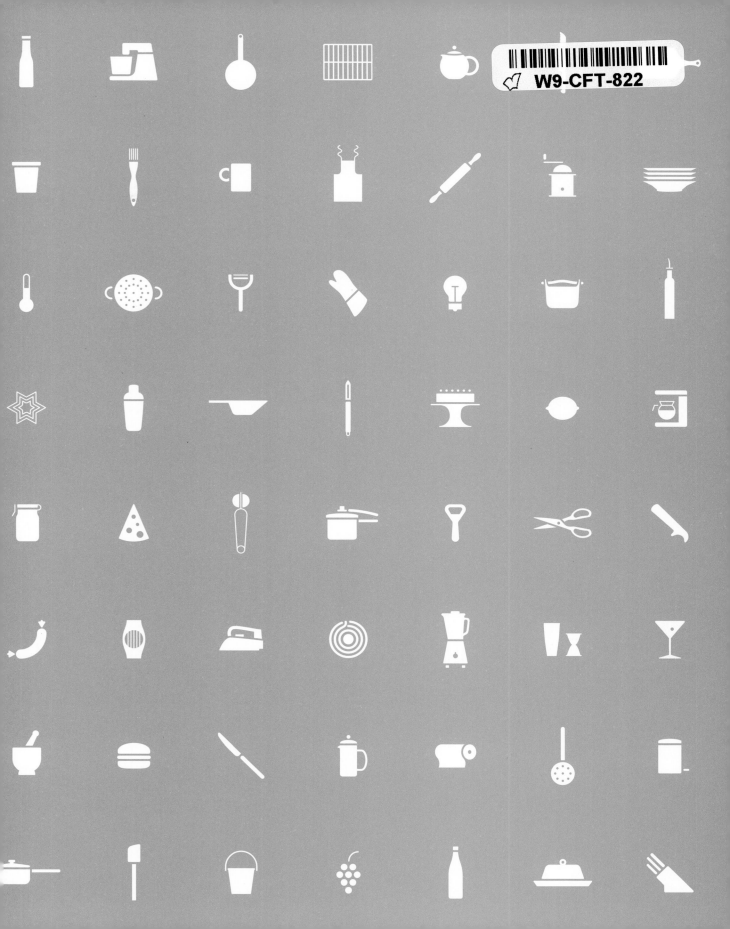

W9-CFT-822

DESIGN AND THE MODERN KITCHEN

counter space

JULIET KINCHIN WITH AIDAN O'CONNOR

The Museum of Modern Art, New York

Table of Contents

Foreword

Counter Space: Design and the Modern Kitchen extends the long commitment of The Museum of Modern Art to the celebration of modernism in every aspect of contemporary life. Throughout the twentieth century the kitchen has been a microcosm for modernist experimentation with new materials, technologies, and ways of living. Pots and pans, teakettles, and laboratory-inspired glass and porcelain kitchenware from the landmark 1934 exhibition *Machine Art* were among the earliest objects of design to enter MoMA's collection, which now encompasses an unparalleled representation of modernist developments in kitchen design over the last hundred years.

The catalyst for *Counter Space*—the first exhibition at MoMA to comprehensively examine the transformation of the modern kitchen—was the recent acquisition by the Museum of a spectacular Frankfurt Kitchen, a highlight of both the show and this publication. This unusually complete example of Austrian architect Margarete Schütte-Lihotzky's 1926-27 iconic design is now the earliest work by a female architect in our collection. Given the prominence of this remarkable acquisition and the relationship between the history of kitchen design and the social history of women, we are proud to present *Counter Space* in association with the publication of *Modern Women: Women Artists at The Museum of Modern Art*, a product of MoMA's Modern Women's Project, which comprises, in addition, a series of exhibitions featuring women artists extending through summer 2011.

Like the most adept of chefs, Juliet Kinchin and Aidan O'Connor have produced a feast for the eyes and mind from a rich and varied array of materials. I am grateful to them and to their many colleagues at the Museum for their contributions to the realization of this multidisciplinary project. On behalf of the staff and trustees of the Museum, I would like to thank Silestone Quartz Surfaces for its generous support of the exhibition and the Nancy Lee and Perry Bass Publication Endowment Fund for making this catalogue possible.

Glenn D. Lowry
Director, The Museum of Modern Art, New York

Charlie Chaplin
and Paulette Goddard
in Modern Times

1936

CHARLES CHAPLIN
(BRITISH, 1889–1977).
MODERN TIMES. 1936. USA

35mm film (black and white, sound), 87 min.

Toward the Modern Kitchen

1

Meal machine, experimental laboratory, status symbol, domestic prison, or the creative and spiritual heart of the home? Over the course of the past century, the kitchen, more than any other room in the modern dwelling, has been radically altered by the technological, social, and aesthetic revolutions of the twentieth century. The modern kitchen epitomizes and embodies its owner's lifestyle and relationship to consumer culture; it also retains its archetypal significance as the symbolic core of the home, the center around which the modern family revolves. It has come to articulate and, at times, actively challenge societal relationships to food, technology, the domestic role of women, and international politics.

Historically, European and American urban kitchens were often drab, dirty places, poorly ventilated and hidden from view. Toward the end of the nineteenth century, however, the kitchen became a central concern of modernism, attracting the attention of architects, domestic reformers, manufacturers, and utility providers. In the context of the late-nineteenth-century Arts and Crafts movement, artists and architects like Richard Riemerschmid turned to humble objects and utilitarian spaces previously ignored by most professional designers. In the 1890s advocates of simplified living began to conceive of the kitchen not as a servant-run domain confined to a basement or annex but as a space central to daily life and social encounters between family and friends. Progressive architects in Europe and the United States designed increasingly compact, sparely furnished environments, often with unified kitchen-living spaces, that took inspiration from modest rural interiors. Many were also involved in the ethnographic recording of such spaces, which were felt to embody national traditions and culture in a purer form than monumental architecture.

It is a mistake to suppose that any room, however small and unpleasantly situated, is "good enough" for a kitchen . . . for upon the results of no other department of woman's domain depend so greatly the health and comfort of the family as upon those involved in this "household workshop."

MRS. E. E. KELLOGG, *SCIENCE IN THE KITCHEN*, 1893

Vinegar Jar with Stopper

c. 1897

RICHARD RIEMERSCHMID
(GERMAN, 1868–1957).
VINEGAR JAR WITH STOPPER.
c. 1897

Glazed stoneware, body: 7⁵/₁₆"
(18.6 cm) high, lid: 1⁵/₈" (4.1 cm)
high. Manufactured by Reinhold
Merkelbach, Grenzhausen,
Germany. Phyllis B. Lambert
Fund, 1958

Perhaps the single most important factor in the transformation of the twentieth-century kitchen was the advent of clean fuels—gas and electricity. The first electric kettle appeared in the 1890s, but the potentially hazardous proximity of water and electricity and the lack of effective electricity distribution networks delayed its widespread acceptance before World War I. Standardization and mass production were also defining elements of the modern kitchen, and they affected everything from interior cabinetwork to the design of food, packaging, and storage containers. The late nineteenth century witnessed a revolution in industrial food processing, starting with coffee, cocoa, and a range of meat and dairy products. Processed foods—such as Tropon, an egg-based protein supplement—and their burgeoning brand identities rapidly transformed traditional patterns of shopping, cooking, and at-home food storage. Factory-line production methods inspired architects such as Frank Lloyd Wright to experiment with the prefabrication of entire homes. Starting in 1911 he produced hundreds of drawings that culminated in the publication of *American System-Built Houses* (c. 1917). The system was based on standardized components that were to be precut in an off-site factory, and it incorporated built-in storage and work surfaces in the kitchen, conceived as part of the prefabricated whole. Despite a marketing campaign, however, there was little interest at the time. It was not until the late 1920s that such concepts would resurface in European design, taken up on a significant scale in housing schemes such as those in Frankfurt.

In the mid-to-late nineteenth century, housework gained new, professional stature and respectability through a domestic-reform movement led by middle-class women. Christine Frederick, Lillian Gilbreth, and Georgie Child were among those in the United States who actively campaigned to rationalize work in the kitchen by applying to the home the principles of scientific management developed by American industrial engineer Frederick Taylor. In the 1920s Christine Frederick—author of the highly influential book *The New Housekeeping* (1912)—established and directed the Applecroft Home Experiment Station from her home in Greenlawn, New York, where she carried out tests of step-saving food preparation processes and investigated 1,800

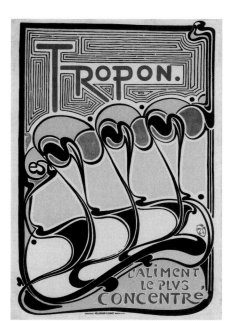

Tropon

1899

**HENRY CLEMENS
VAN DE VELDE**
(BELGIAN, 1863–1957).
*TROPON, L'ALIMENT
LE PLUS CONCENTRÉ*
(TROPON, THE MOST
CONCENTRATED
NOURISHMENT). POSTER
ADVERTISING PROTEIN
EXTRACT. 1899

Lithograph, 44 x 30³/₈"
(111.8 x 77.2 cm).
Printed by Hollerbaum
& Schmidt, Berlin. Arthur
Drexler Fund, 1988

Coffee and Tea Box

1928–30

JACOB JONGERT
(DUTCH, 1883–1942).
COFFEE AND TEA BOX.
1928–30

Printed tin, 14 ½ x 16 ⁹⁄₁₆ x
11 ¼" (36.8 x 43 x 28.6 cm).
Purchase, 1992

Electric Kettle

1909

PETER BEHRENS
(GERMAN, 1868–1940).
ELECTRIC KETTLE. 1909

Nickel-plated brass and
rattan, 9 x 8 ¾ x 6 ¼"
(22.9 x 22.2 x 15.9 cm).
Manufactured by Allgemeine
Elektrizitäts Gesellschaft,
Frankfurt. Gift of Manfred
Ludewig, 1992

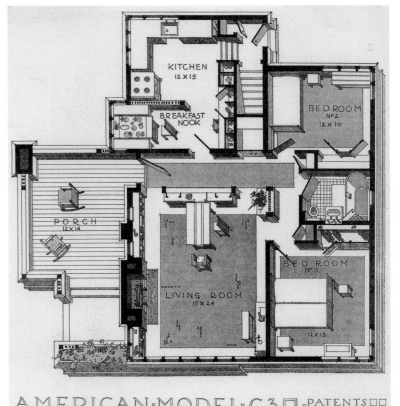

American System–Built Houses

c. 1915–17

FRANK LLOYD WRIGHT
(AMERICAN, 1867–1959).
AMERICAN SYSTEM-BUILT
HOUSES FOR THE RICHARDS
COMPANY, MILWAUKEE,
WISCONSIN. PROJECT. PLAN
OF MODEL C3. c. 1915–17

Lithograph, 11 x 8 ½"
(27.9 x 21.6 cm). Gift of David
Rockefeller, Jr., Fund, Ira
Howard Levy Fund, and Jeffrey
P. Klein Purchase Fund, 1993

Christine Frederick in her Applecroft Home Experiment Station

c. 1912–14

CHRISTINE FREDERICK
(RIGHT) IN HER
APPLECROFT HOME
EXPERIMENT STATION
CONFERRING WITH
"HOME MOTION" STUDY
PARTICIPANTS: AN
EVALUATOR (CENTER)
AND A HOME COOK
(LEFT), GREENLAWN,
NEW YORK, c. 1912–14

Schlesinger Library,
Radcliffe Institute,
Harvard University,
Cambridge,
Massachusetts

Diagrams from The New Housekeeping

1914

DIAGRAMS FROM
THE NEW HOUSEKEEPING:
EFFICIENCY STUDIES
IN HOME MANAGEMENT
BY CHRISTINE FREDERICK
(NEW YORK: 1914). FIRST
EDITION 1912

Library of The Museum of
Modern Art, New York

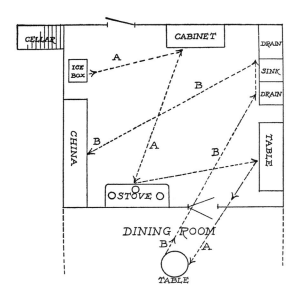

Diagram showing badly arranged equipment, which makes confused intersecting chains of steps, in either preparing or clearing away a meal. (A–preparing; B–clearing)

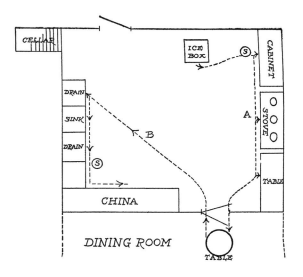

Diagram showing proper arrangement of equipment, which makes a simple chain of steps, in either preparing or clearing away a meal. (A–preparing; B–clearing)

IRWIN GERSHEN
(AMERICAN). **GERSHEN-
NEWARK** (USA). SHRIMP
CLEANER. 1954

Plastic and metal, 8 ½ x 3 ¼
x ¾" (21.6 x 8.3 x 1.9 cm).
Manufactured by Plastic
Dispensers Inc., Newark,
New Jersey. Department
Purchase, 1956

different products, from household appliances to foodstuffs. Margarete (Grete) Schütte-Lihotzky, the first woman to qualify as an architect in her native Vienna, described Frederick's book as her bible. In 1926-27 she designed one of modernism's most famous cooking spaces—the Frankfurt Kitchen, part of a massive public housing effort in Germany.

It was the acquisition in 2009 by The Museum of Modern Art, New York, of a complete example of Schütte-Lihotzky's iconic Frankfurt Kitchen (now the earliest work by a female architect in MoMA's collection) that inspired the *Counter Space* project. The interrelationship of the arts was a founding premise of the Museum; in addition to its representation by architecture and industrial design, images of the modern kitchen in film, photography, and graphic arts have been in MoMA's collection since the institution's early years. Beginning with *Machine Art,* in 1934, popular exhibitions have featured kitchenware, including pots and pans as well as more obscure innovations, such as the Gershen-Newark shrimp cleaner of 1954. In addition, the delights and nightmares of this hub of domestic activity—experienced by some as a pleasantly sensual place but by others as claustrophobic, messy, and dangerous—have provided a rich vein of subject matter for artists since the late 1960s that is also represented in the collection.

This book chronicles the innovations of Schütte-Lihotzky's generation and demonstrates, through architecture, design objects, and works of art from the Museum's collection, how they were extended and modified during the consumer revolution and Cold War that followed World War II. In so doing it reveals the modern kitchen as a theater of social, cultural, and political debate that also continues to recapitulate the key tenets of modern architecture and industrial design in microcosm. Combining pragmatic applications of new materials and technologies with the articulation of more poetic, flexible, and diversified responses to contemporary lifestyles, the design of the modern kitchen exemplifies the vivid realization of art in daily life.

Kitchen in the Haus am Horn

1923

BENITA OTTE (GERMAN, 1892–1976). **ERNST GEBHARDT** (GERMAN). KITCHEN IN THE HAUS AM HORN EXPERIMENTAL HOUSE, BAUHAUS EXHIBITION, WEIMAR, 1923. CERAMICS DESIGNED BY **THEODOR BOGLER** (GERMAN, 1897–1968)

As illustrated in *Ein Versuchhaus des Bauhauses in Weimar: Haus am Horn* (An Experimental House by the Bauhaus in Weimar: Haus am Horn), by Adolf Meyer (1925)

KÜCHE   AUFWASCHTISCH, SCHRANK, ARBEITSTISCH

The New Kitchen

2

Following World War I, kitchens, long ignored by design professionals, began to attract unprecedented attention from social reformers, progressive architects, manufacturers, and utility suppliers, all intent on transforming spaces that were drab, unsanitary, and hidden from view. The "New Kitchen," epitomized by Grete Schütte-Lihotzky's Frankfurt Kitchen of 1926–27, was rationally planned and industrially produced for popular consumption. Simplified house plans and the innovative use of prefabricated construction, combined with a desire to vanquish drudgery and optimize efficiency, resulted in compact, practical spaces central to the functioning of the modern home.

The New Kitchen was shaped significantly by research into new materials and technologies between the two world wars. Aluminum and heat-resistant glass led to the development of exciting new products, and the increased availability of electricity and gas revolutionized appliance design. Large companies, especially in the United States, established modern test kitchens, employing professional home economists to collaborate with industrial designers on innovative products for expanding markets.

From Moscow and Prague to Brussels and Berlin, kitchens were at the core of radical projects to modernize housing and renew cities. Whether conceived as a galley for food preparation or a collective facility outside the home, these variants of the New Kitchen shared an admiration for scientific reason and utopian aspirations for a more egalitarian society. Transformation of daily life at the level of the kitchen, it was argued, would be followed by behavioral change and improved social well-being. During the Great Depression similar concerns informed Franklin D. Roosevelt's promotion of modern kitchens in the United States as part of the New Deal. World War II followed, and the emphasis on hygiene, health, and the economical use of resources intrinsic to the New Kitchen was crucial to the home front on both sides of the conflict.

The modern kitchen has become a model workshop, a chemical laboratory. . . . It is the best designed and most rationalized room of the modern house.

KAREL TEIGE, *THE MINIMUM DWELLING*, 1932

Kitchen Storage Pot

1923

Designed by Bogler in the ceramics workshops of the Bauhaus, the robust, simple form of this earthenware pot reflects the conviction at the school that basic geometric shapes were well suited to industrial production. The pot was slip-cast from a plaster mold, a method of mass producing ceramics. Given the depressed state of the economy and the uneven quality of the prototypes, however, the pot was never licensed for large-scale manufacture, despite initial interest at trade fairs in Frankfurt and Leipzig.

THEODOR BOGLER
(GERMAN, 1897–1968).
KITCHEN STORAGE POT.
1923

Earthenware with metallic glaze, body: 5 ¼ x 6 ¾" diam. (13.3 x 17.1 cm), lid: 1 ⅜ x 5 ¼" diam. (3.5 x 13.3 cm). Manufactured by Bauhaus Ceramics Workshops, Dornburg, Germany. Estée and Joseph Lauder Design Fund, 1970

Home Building and Town Planning

1928-30

The split view on this exhibition poster demonstrates the importance attached to the kitchen in the design of affordable modern housing. The devastation and extreme deprivation in Vienna that followed World War I radicalized many architects and designers, inspiring them to engage with class politics and, on a more practical level, to confront the city's chronic housing shortage. Grete Schütte-Lihotzky became involved with the Gesellschafts- und Wirtschaftsmuseum (Museum of Society and Business), an organization established in 1924 to foster awareness of the relationship among design, the urban environment, and social well-being using informational graphics such as this poster.

ATTRIBUTED TO
GERD ARNTZ (GERMAN, 1900–1988). *WOHNUNG UND STÄDTEBAU* (HOME BUILDING AND TOWN PLANNING). 1928-30. POSTER FOR A PERMANENT EXHIBITION AT THE GESELLSCHAFTS- UND WIRTSCHAFTSMUSEUM (MUSEUM OF SOCIETY AND BUSINESS), VIENNA

Letterpress, 13 7/16 x 14 9/16"
(34.1 x 37 cm). Printed by Münster & Co., Vienna. Jan Tschichold Collection. Gift of Philip Johnson, 1999

GEWERBEMUSEUM BASEL
9. FEBRUAR – 16. MÄRZ 1930

DIE
PRAKTISCHE
KÜCHE

TÄGLICH 14–19 UHR
SONNTAG 10–12
14–19 UHR
EINTRITT FREI

GRAPH. ANSTALT
W. WASSERMANN

The
Practical
Kitchen

1930

In the late 1920s and the 1930s, kitchens were highlighted in many modern architecture exhibitions. This poster for an exhibition in Basel is dominated by an axonometric rendering of a miniscule kitchen by Swiss architect Rudolf Preiswerk. In the exhibition, visitors could see a full-scale model of the same design, which had a footprint little more than thirty-seven square feet (3.4 square meters). In the accompanying catalogue, German design reformer Erna Meyer identified such compact and ergonomic arrangements as the most important trend in modern kitchen design.

HELENE HAASBAUER-WALLRATH (SWISS, 1885–1968). *DIE PRAKTISCHE KÜCHE* (THE PRACTICAL KITCHEN). 1930. POSTER FOR AN EXHIBITION AT THE GEWERBEMUSEUM, BASEL

Offset lithograph, 50 x 35½" (127 x 90.2 cm). Purchase, 2010

Tea Cart

1928

MARCEL BREUER (AMERICAN, BORN HUNGARY. 1902–1981). TEA CART (MODEL B54). 1928

Nickel-plated tubular steel, rubber, and painted wood, 30½ x 34⅝ x 21½" (77.5 x 88 x 54.6 cm). Manufactured by Thonet, Vienna. Estée and Joseph Lauder Design Fund, 1981

WERKBUNDAUSSTELLUNG
DIE WOHNUNG
JULI-OKT.
STUTTGART 1927

Werkbund Exhibition, The Dwelling

1927

KARL LUDWIG STRAUB
(GERMAN, BORN 1900).
*WERKBUND AUSSTELLUNG,
DIE WOHNUNG* (WERKBUND
EXHIBITION, THE DWELLING).
1927. POSTER FOR AN
EXHIBITION IN STUTTGART

Offset lithograph, 23-3/8 x
16-5/8" (59.4 x 42.2 cm).
Special Purchase Fund, 1937

The Deutscher Werkbund, a forward-looking association of manufacturers, designers, and architects, helped position Germany at the forefront of the development of the rational kitchen. An international exhibition organized under its auspices in Stuttgart in 1927 took the form of a modern housing estate, exemplifying an admiration for scientific rationale and efficiency. Architects and experts on home economics collaborated on kitchen design; Walter Gropius, director of the Bauhaus, and Dutch architect J. J. Pieter Oud took advice on the layout and equipment of kitchens from Erna Meyer (the latter had published the hugely popular book *Der neue Haushalt* [The New Housekeeping] in 1926). The site featured terraced houses designed by Grete Schütte-Lihotzky and a Frankfurt Kitchen, which she exhibited to international acclaim.

Welkut
Poultry Shears

1909-43

J. A. HENCKELS (GERMANY, EST. 1731). WELKUT POULTRY SHEARS. 1909-43

Chromium-plated steel, 10¼" (26 cm) long. Manufactured by J. A. Henckels, Solingen, Germany, and USA. Gift of Fifth Avenue Cutlery Shop Inc., 1943

Minimal
Dwelling

c. 1928

ALBRECHT HEUBNER (GERMAN, 1908-1945). MINIMAL DWELLING. PROJECT. c. 1928

Cut-and-pasted printed papers, gouache, and graphite on paper, 11¾ x 14¾" (29.9 x 37.4 cm). Acquired through Walter Gropius, 1977

Frankfurt Kitchen

1926-27

MARGARETE
SCHÜTTE-LIHOTZKY
(AUSTRIAN, 1897–2000).
FRANKFURT KITCHEN.
1926–27

View toward the window,
as illustrated in *Das neue
Frankfurt* 1, no. 5 (1927)

The Frankfurt Kitchen

The New Dwelling sets for its occupants the task of rethinking everything afresh, organizing a new lifestyle, and of winning freedom from the irrelevant clutter of outmoded habits of thought and old-fashioned equipment.

FRANZ SCHUSTER, *DAS NEUE FRANKFURT* 1, NO. 5 (1927)

War and inflation precipitated a housing crisis in the 1920s in all major German cities. In Frankfurt the response was an ambitious program, known as "The New Frankfurt," that encompassed the construction of affordable public housing and modern amenities throughout the city. At the core of the transformation was a 1926–27 kitchen design by Grete Schütte-Lihotzky. The Frankfurt Kitchen, as it was known, was conceived as one of the first steps toward a better, more egalitarian world.

Under the overall direction of Ernst May, director of the Frankfurt Municipal Building Department, the housing program and kitchens became testing grounds for standardization and modern industrial production. The aim was to keep monthly rentals, including basic utilities—gas, electricity, hot running water, and radio reception—and fully equipped kitchens, within the reach of the lowest-paid workers. Economies of scale were applied to the manufacture of more than fifteen thousand housing units, using standardized precast concrete panels as the basic building blocks. Within five years, more than ten percent of Frankfurt's population was living in newly designed housing and communities.

Schütte-Lihotzky was the first woman to qualify as an architect in her native Austria and the only female in the international team of architects May assembled. Reminiscing about her decision to study architecture, Schütte-Lihotzky remarked that "in 1916 no one would have conceived of a woman being commissioned to build a house—not even myself." Inspired by her mentor at the Vienna School of Applied Arts, Oskar Strnad, she became involved in designing affordable housing and worked

Ginnheim-Höhenblick Housing Estate, Frankfurt

1928

As illustrated in *Das neue Frankfurt* 3, no. 7/8 (July/August 1928). Photograph by Wolff. MoMA's Frankfurt Kitchen was salvaged from the second floor of the house on the corner in 1993.

with another Viennese architect, Adolf Loos, on planning settlements for World War I veterans. Impressed by the functional clarity that she applied to housing problems and kitchen design in these projects, May invited her to join his Frankfurt department in 1926. That Schütte-Lihotzky was to design the kitchens helped promote the modernization of housing in Frankfurt to those who viewed cooking and cleaning as women's work, but, she pointed out, "The truth of the matter was, I'd never run a household before designing the Frankfurt Kitchen, I'd never cooked, and had no idea about cooking."

After reading the first German edition of *The New Housekeeping: Efficiency Studies in Home Management,* by Christine Frederick, in 1921 Schütte-Lihotzky had become convinced that "women's struggle for economic independence and personal develop-ment meant that the rationalization of housework was an absolute necessity." Rethinking the kitchen was part of organizing a new lifestyle, free from "irrelevant clutter," that would reduce the burden of women's labor in the home. "The problem of organizing the daily work of the housewife in a systematic manner is equally important for all classes of society," Schütte-Lihotzky wrote in 1926. "To achieve this, the arrangement of the kitchen and its relationship to the other rooms in the dwelling must be considered first."

The Frankfurt Kitchen was designed like a laboratory or factory, based on contemporary theories about efficiency, hygiene, and workflow as well as detailed time-motion studies and interviews Schütte-Lihotzky conducted with housewives and women's groups. In addition, she looked to professional cooking spaces such as railroad kitchens and ships' galleys as models of efficiency and compact planning. The Frankfurt Kitchen was planned for food preparation and cleanup, with a sliding door that opened to the living-dining area. Each kitchen came complete with a revolving stool, a gas stove, built-in storage, a foldaway ironing board, an adjustable ceiling light, and a removable garbage drawer. Labeled aluminum storage bins provided tidy organization for staples like sugar and rice as well as easy pouring. Careful thought was given to materials for specific functions, such as oak flour containers (to repel

Aluminum Pouring Bins

1926-27

MARGARETE
SCHÜTTE-LIHOTZKY
(AUSTRIAN, 1897-2000).
ALUMINUM POURING
BINS FROM A FRANKFURT
KITCHEN. 1926-27

Aluminum, each: 5 ½ x 4 ¼
x 11" (14 x 10.8 x 27.9 cm).
Manufactured by Haarer,
Frankfurt. Gift of Astrid
Debus-Steinberg, 2010

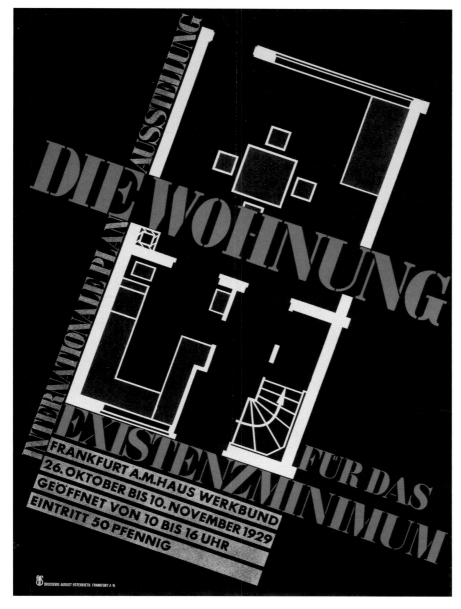

The Dwelling for Minimal Living

1929

HANS LEISTIKOW
(GERMAN, 1892-1962).
*DIE WOHNUNG FÜR
DAS EXISTENZMINIMUM*
(THE DWELLING FOR
MINIMAL LIVING). 1929.
POSTER FOR EXHIBITION,
CONGRÈS INTERNATIONAL
D'ARCHITECTURE (CIAM)
CONFERENCE, FRANKFURT

Offset lithograph, 46 x 33"
(116.8 x 84.0 cm). Printed by
Druckerei August Osterrieth,
Frankfurt. Gift of The Lauder
Foundation, Leonard and
Evelyn Lauder Fund, 1980

mealworms) and beech cutting surfaces (to resist staining and knife marks). Ten to twelve thousand Frankfurt Kitchens were manufactured in three basic models, each with minor variations. The type in MoMA's collection was the most common and least costly.

Ernst May was an energetic publicist. At a 1929 conference of modernist architects held in Frankfurt, international attention focused on his modernization program. Of the housing plans submitted by delegates for the concurrent exhibition, an example incorporating the outline of a Frankfurt Kitchen was taken to epitomize the conference's theme of "Minimal Living." In 1930, at the request of the Soviet Russian government, May led a "building brigade," including Schütte-Lihotzky, to implement the lessons of Frankfurt on an even larger scale in the planning of new industrial towns in the USSR. She remains best known for the Frankfurt Kitchen, but Schütte-Lihotzky's achievements as an architect in the Soviet Union, Turkey, and Austria were more varied. During World War II her career was interrupted by four years in prison for her activities in the anti-Nazi resistance movement. During the Cold War that followed, her professional opportunities in Austria were limited because of her continued membership in the Communist Party.

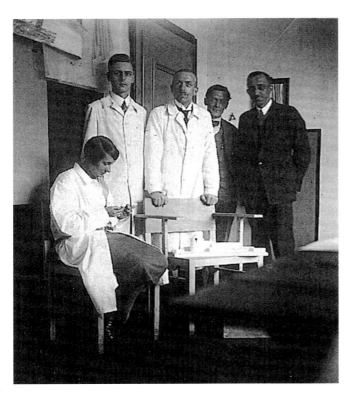

Margarete Schütte-Lihotzky with colleagues from the Frankfurt Municipal Building Department

c. 1928

University of Applied
Arts, Vienna

Plan of the Frankfurt Kitchen indicating its labor-saving features

1927

DIAGRAM FROM *NEJEMŠI BYT*
(THE MINIMUM DWELLING),
BY KAREL TEIGE (1932)

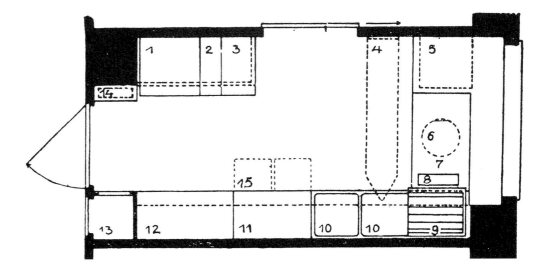

1. GAS STOVE
2. COUNTERTOP
3. COOK BOX
4. FOLD-DOWN IRONING BOARD
5. FOOD CUPBOARD

6. SWIVEL STOOL
7. WORK SURFACE
8. GARBAGE DRAWER
9. DRAINING BOARD
10. SINK

11. ALUMINIUM STORAGE BINS
12. CUPBOARD FOR POTS AND PANS
13. BROOM CLOSET
14. HEATER
15. PULL-OUT BOARD

Frankfurt Kitchen

1926-27

MARGARETE SCHÜTTE-LIHOTZKY
(AUSTRIAN, 1897-2000).
FRANKFURT KITCHEN
FROM THE GINNHEIM-
HÖHENBLICK HOUSING
ESTATE, FRANKFURT.
1926-27

Installation view of *Counter Space: Design and the Modern Kitchen,* The Museum of Modern Art, New York, September 15, 2010–May 2, 2011. 8' 9" x 12' 10" x 6' 10" (266.7 x 391.2 x 208.3 cm). Gift of Joan R. Brewster in memory of her husband George W. W. Brewster, by exchange, and the Architecture & Design Purchase Fund, 2009

Apartment for a Single Person

1931

In her design of several kitchens for the show *Die Wohnung unserer Zeit* (The Dwelling of Our Time) at the 1931 Deutsche Bauausstellung (German Building Exhibition) in Berlin, Reich embraced the rational principles of domestic reformers Christine Frederick and Erna Meyer. Reich's Apartment for a Single Person featured a cooking cabinet that was subsequently put into production by Otto Kahn, a banker and influential patron of the arts. When closed it appeared to be an ordinary closet or wardrobe, but opening it revealed a sink, shelves, two burners, drawers, counter space, and a hook on which to hang a kettle.

LILLY REICH (GERMAN, 1885–1947). APARTMENT FOR A SINGLE PERSON. 1931. VIEW OF LIVING ROOM AND COOKING CUPBOARD AS INSTALLED AT *DIE WOHNUNG UNSERER ZEIT* (THE DWELLING OF OUR TIME), DEUTSCHE BAUAUSSTELLUNG (GERMAN BUILDING EXHIBITION). BERLIN

Gelatin silver print, 6 5/8 x 9" (16.8 x 22.9 cm). Mies van der Rohe Archive, gift of the architect, 1937

The unadorned geometric forms of these popular Kubus containers make them the kind of mass-produced objects that the Bauhaus had aspired to produce. Stackable, modular, space saving, and hygienic, they could be transferred directly from refrigerator or cupboard to the dining table, and encouraged the thrifty use of leftovers. Wagenfeld designed them three years after being appointed art director of the large glassware manufacturer Vereinigte Lausitzer Glaswerke.

Kubus Stacking Storage Containers

1938

WILHELM WAGENFELD
(GERMAN, 1900-1990).
KUBUS STACKING STORAGE
CONTAINERS. 1938

Molded glass, smallest: ½ x
3 ½ x 3 ⅝" (1.3 x 8.9 x 9.2 cm),
largest: 3 ¼ x 7 ¼ x 7 ¼" (8.3 x
18.4 x 18.4 cm). Manufactured
by Vereinigte Lausitzer
Glaswerke AG, Weisswasser,
Germany. Mrs. Armand P.
Bartos Fund, 1990

Gas Cooks,
Heats, Freezes

1928

In 1923 more than 100,000 visitors flocked to the first Salon des Arts Ménagers (Exhibition of Household Arts) in Paris to admire modern kitchens, vacuum cleaners, and other domestic innovations. The aims of the salon were both educational and commercial, in keeping with similar fairs established in other European centers at the time. This poster was commissioned for the 1928 salon by a society promoting the development of the French gas industry. Dramatically highlighting the valve, Bernard focused attention on the simple gesture required to release gas for purposes of cooking, heating, and refrigeration.

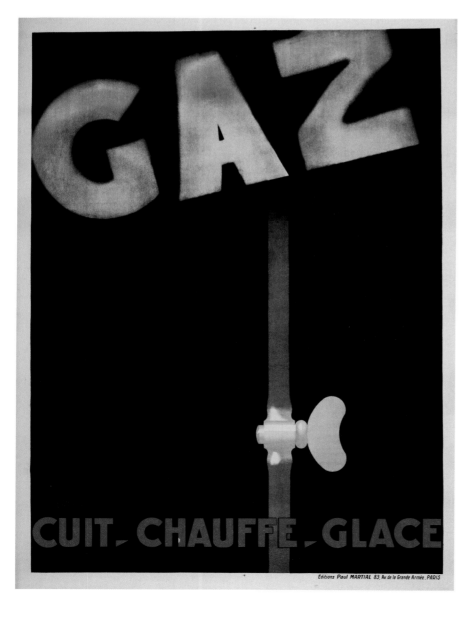

FRANCIS BERNARD
(FRENCH, 1900–1979). *GAZ CUIT, CHAUFFE, GLACE* (GAS COOKS, HEATS, FREEZES). 1928

Offset lithograph, 63 x 47¼" (160 x 120 cm). Printed by Paul Martail, Paris. Department Purchase Funds, 1987

Rayograph

1922

In keeping with the prevalent spirit of New Objectivity, Man Ray
subjected a humble kitchen grater and strainer to rigorous scrutiny.
The utilitarian forms are rendered ghostly and mysterious by
means of a technique that involved placing the object on light-
sensitive paper. Man Ray experimented with such photograms
after moving to Paris in 1921. He dubbed the results of his efforts
"Rayographs"—a play on his name but also a twist on the Latin
roots of the word *photograph*, meaning "light writing."

By the 1930s, Coors Porcelain Company was one of the world's largest producers of chemical porcelain, a material developed from experimentation with silicate compounds. Heat and scratch resistant, the material was well suited for both industrial and domestic use. The company had strong links with Germany, where one of its directors had received his training as a chemist, and many of the Coors vessel shapes that became popular in American kitchens were replicas of German laboratory ware, which had been banned from importation to the United States in 1915 as part of a trade embargo.

COORS PORCELAIN CO.
(USA, EST. 1910).
BEAKERS. 1920s

Glazed porcelain, largest:
8 ³⁄₈ x 5 ³⁄₈" diam. (21.2 x
13.7 cm). Manufactured
by Coors Porcelain Co.,
Golden, Colorado. Gift of
the manufacturer, 1934

Coors Porcelain Beakers

1920s

Installation view of *Machine Art*, The Museum of Modern Art, New York, March 7–31, 1934. Archives of The Museum of Modern Art, New York

View of Machine Art, The Museum of Modern Art, New York

1934

In this grand, three-floor exhibition organized by Philip Johnson, ball bearings, propellers, springs, laboratory equipment, and kitchenware—including objects by such well-known American manufacturers as Corning Glass Works, The Aluminum Cooking Utensil Company, Coors Porcelain, and Revere Copper and Brass—were displayed on pedestals against white walls, given the unprecedented status of art. The first objects of design to enter the Museum's collection were selected from this show.

Salt and Pepper Shakers

c. 1935

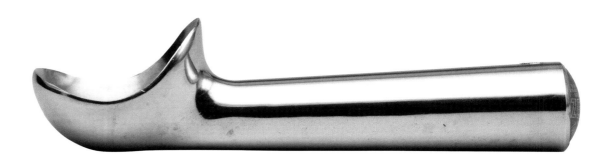

WILLIAM LESCAZE
(AMERICAN, BORN
SWITZERLAND. 1896-
1969). SALT AND PEPPER
SHAKERS. c. 1935

Aluminum and plastic, each:
1³⁄₄ x 2 x ⁵⁄₈" (4.4 x 5.1 x
1.6 cm). Manufactured by
Revere Copper and Brass
Inc., Rome, New York.
Dorothy Cullman Purchase
Fund, 2002

Ice Cream
Scoop

1935

SHERMAN L. KELLY
(AMERICAN, 1869-1952).
ICE CREAM SCOOP. 1935

Cast aluminum, 1³⁄₄ x 7" (4.4
x 17.8 cm). Manufactured by
Roll Dippers Inc. (formerly
the Zeroll Co.), Maumee,
Ohio. Purchase Fund, 1956

Presto Cheese Slicer

c. 1940

JOHN CARROLL
(AMERICAN, 1892–1958).
PRESTO CHEESE SLICER.
c. 1940

Cast aluminum and steel
wire, 4 ½ x 3 ¾" (11.4 x
9.5 cm). Manufactured by
R. A. Frederick Co., USA.
Gift of Edgar Kaufmann, Jr.,
1946

Vegetable Peeler

c. 1944

EKCO PRODUCTS CO.
(USA, EST. 1888).
VEGETABLE PEELER.
c. 1944

Steel, 6 ⅞ x ⅞ x ½" (17.5 x
2.2 x 1.3 cm). Manufactured
by Ekco Products Co.,
Chicago. Purchase, 1956

A Better Home

RURAL ELECTRIFICATION ADMINISTRATION
U. S. Department of Agriculture

LESTER BEALL
(AMERICAN, 1903-1969).
A BETTER HOME. 1937-41.
POSTER FOR THE RURAL
ELECTRIFICATION
ADMINISTRATION, UNITED
STATES DEPARTMENT
OF AGRICULTURE

Offset lithograph and
screenprint, 40 x 30"
(101.6 x 76.2 cm). Gift of
the designer, 2010

A Better Home

1937-41

The core message of Beall's poster is simple: electrification
of the kitchen will improve the home and (signaled by the
patriotic color scheme) promote a more cohesive society.
As part of President Roosevelt's New Deal program, the Rural
Electrification Administration was created in 1935 to bring
electricity to impoverished areas, where as few as ten percent
of homes had electric power. Public officials recognized the
effectiveness of commercial advertising strategies—such as
this poster—in their mission to convince rural housewives of
the benefits of switching from wood, coal, and oil to electricity.

Magnalite Teakettle

1936

To counter faltering sales during the Great Depression, more adventurous manufacturers began to employ outside design consultants and invest in materials research. Among them was the Wagner Manufacturing Company—known for its traditional cast-iron cookware—which introduced Magnalite, a patented aluminum alloy, in the early 1930s. Rideout, one of a new generation of American industrial designers, was brought in to rework the appearance of the company's products, including this teakettle. Here his efforts were focused on aesthetics more than functionality: the kettle's lid is semi-permanently attached and may only be removed by first detaching the handle with a screwdriver.

JOHN G. RIDEOUT
(AMERICAN, 1898-1951).
MAGNALITE TEAKETTLE.
1936

Aluminum/copper/nickel/
magnesium alloy (Magnalite),
and lacquered wood, 8 ½
x 9 ¹³/₁₆" diam. (21.6 x 25 cm).
Manufactured by Wagner
Mfg. Co., Sidney, Ohio.
Purchase fund, 1944

Wear-Ever Rotary Food Press

1929–34

**THE ALUMINUM
COOKING UTENSIL CO.**
(USA, EST. 1901).
WEAR-EVER ROTARY
FOOD PRESS. 1929–34

Aluminum, steel, and wood,
9 x 11 ³⁄₈" diam. (22.9 x
28.9 cm) Manufactured by
The Aluminum Cooking
Utensil Co., New York. Gift
of Lewis & Conger, 1947

Revere Covered Saucepan

1938–39

In 1937, after a year of intensive experimentation, Revere
Copper and Brass successfully developed a method of adhering
a copper deposit to a stainless-steel vessel by means of
electroplating. The result was a compound that resisted
corrosion by food acids and conducted heat effectively and
uniformly. At the same time, the designers refined the balance
of the pans and devised a rivet-free construction. The result,
Revere Ware, was launched at the first International House-
wares Show, in Chicago in 1939. It took off after World War II,
when metals were no longer being diverted to the war effort.

W. ARCHIBALD WELDEN
(AMERICAN, 1900–1970).
COVERED SAUCEPAN.
1938–39

Stainless steel with copper
bottom, 5 ¹⁄₂ x 7 ¹⁄₂" diam.
(14 x 19 cm). Manufactured by
Revere Copper and Brass Inc.,
Rome, New York. Gift of the
Education Department, 1954

Universal
Pressure Cooker

1945

The first saucepan-style pressure cooker was launched at the 1939 World's Fair in New York, and this new product type rapidly gained popularity throughout the United States and Europe. Like that first example, this pressure cooker enabled reduced cooking times while preserving food's vitamin and mineral content. Landers, Frary & Clark, which had used the trade name "Universal" since the 1890s, manufactured an increasingly diverse range of metal products for the modern kitchen under the moniker, from mousetraps and percolators to can openers, electric ranges, and aluminum cookware.

WILLIAM J. RUSSELL
(AMERICAN). UNIVERSAL
PRESSURE COOKER. 1945

Aluminum, steel, and plastic,
7 ½ x 8 ½" diam. (19 x 21.6 cm)
Manufactured by Landers,
Frary & Clark, New Britain,
Connecticut. Gift of
the manufacturer, 1946

Cookie
Cutters

c. 1940

UNKNOWN DESIGNER.
COOKIE CUTTERS. c. 1940

Tin, 3 ¼ x 3 ¼ x 3 ¼" (8.3 x
8.3 x 8.3 cm). Purchase, 1942

Corning Glass Works (first known as Brooklyn Flint Glass Works) was a successful producer of glass for electric lighting and railroad signal lanterns through the early twentieth century; after years of research, it made a huge break into the domestic market in 1915 with Pyrex (heat-resistant borosilicate glass). In 1919, over 4.5 million pieces of Pyrex were sold in the United States, including bakingware still popular today. This frying pan is part of the Flameware line of products, introduced in 1936, which can withstand direct flame and therefore be used on the stovetop, a feature that achieved additional significance once metals were rationed during World War II. Made familiar to shoppers by companion literature prepared by Corning home economists, Flameware remained in production until 1979.

CORNING GLASS WORKS
(USA, EST. 1851). COMPANY
DESIGN. FRYING PAN. c. 1942

Borosilicate glass (Pyrex) and
steel, overall: 2¾ x 12½ x 7"
diam. (7 x 31.8 x 17.8 cm).
Manufactured by Corning Glass
Works, Corning, New York.
Purchase. 1948

Corning Frying Pan

c. 1942

Kitchen of Tomorrow

1944

"The 'Kitchen of Tomorrow' that does everything but put out the cat at night now makes its debut," declared one Philadelphia newspaper. Three full-scale models of this prototype kitchen (designed to foster consumer demand at a time when the end of World War II seemed imminent) were reportedly seen by more than 1.6 million people in major department stores across the country; visitors could vote for the features they wanted to see realized. Cooking was done in glass-topped recessed vessels that eliminated pots and pans. Sliding panels covered the sink, cooking unit, and automatic food mixer, so when not in use these units became part of a long buffet, "ready for use as a study bench for the children or a bar for dad."

H. ALBERT CRESTON DONER
(AMERICAN, 1903-1991).
**LIBBEY-OWENS-FORD GLASS
COMPANY** (USA). KITCHEN
OF TOMORROW. 1944

Gelatin silver prints, each:
8¾ x 7" (22.2 x 17.8 cm).
Architecture and Design Study
Collection. Photographs by
Hedrich-Blessing Studio,
Chicago

The thrifty aesthetics and labor-saving ethos of the New Kitchen came to the fore during World War II. Merchant shipping was targeted by German U-boats, disrupting importation of food into Britain that had previously amounted to 55 million tons a year. From the outset of the war, the mandatory rationing of food, resources, and furnishings was an ever-present concern. Through posters commissioned from leading commercial artists of the day, the Ministry of Information conveyed the vital need for food conservation, home gardening, and the elimination of vermin from the kitchen.

British World War II Propaganda Posters

c. 1941–43

Parsons Pureaire Unit Kitchen

c. 1950

THE PARSONS CO. (USA).
PUBLICITY PHOTO FOR
PARSONS PUREAIRE UNIT
KITCHEN (DETAIL). c. 1950
Gelatin silver print, 9 ¼
x 7 ½" (23.5 x 19.1 cm).
Architecture and Design
Study Collection

Visions of Plenty

3

"America represents the fat kitchen, and Europe a very lean kitchen indeed." This is how German émigré Heinrich Hauser, writing in 1945, described the "spiritual chasm" opening up between the two regions. While rationing and postwar reconstruction maintained a hold on Europe, the United States' economy experienced a significant boom and rapidly came to dominate the world market in consumer goods. Building on wartime research into materials, technologies, and ergonomics, large American companies such as General Electric, Westinghouse, Hotpoint, and Rubbermaid shaped powerful corporate identities, reinforced by advertisements in the new medium of television.

A climate of abundance and an emphasis on consumer choice, embraced in the United States during the Cold War as hallmarks of capitalism and democracy, put a new spin on the well-established rhetoric of efficiency and anti-drudgery in design for the kitchen. Members of "the affluent society" (as economist John Kenneth Galbraith referred to a segment of Americans) could acquire for their kitchens—increasingly suburban and spacious—an ever-expanding range of products, available from the mid-1950s in new shopping malls.

Due in part to American aid administered through the Marshall Plan, design powers soon reemerged in Europe. In Germany, Braun developed a cohesive family of appliances revered internationally for their superior functionality and pure form. Italy became a hotbed of innovative design in plastics, and in the 1960s designers such as Virgilio Forchiassin reimagined the kitchen in mobile and miniaturized forms. By the 1970s, alternative design had pushed beyond new materials and forms to consider social and environmental concerns. In Sweden, Ergonomi Design shaped kitchen tools for people with disabilities and the elderly, while Yemeni diplomat Adnan Tarcici supported sustainable energy with impressively simple solar cookers. Throughout the 1980s, 1990s, and 2000s, designers have continued to creatively address the enormous range of materials, functions, possibilities, and problems that reside in the modern kitchen.

In the '30s and '40s it was fashionable to compress the kitchen into a space-saving, antiseptic cubicle. . . . Since the war, whole houses are virtually being designed around colorful, labor-saving kitchens that can also serve as all-purpose living space for the family.

"KITCHEN COMEBACK," *TIME* MAGAZINE, 1954

GARDNER SOULE. "NEW
KITCHEN BUILT TO FIT YOUR
WIFE." *POPULAR SCIENCE*
(SEPTEMBER 1953): 172-73.

Tall, short or medium-sized, she's bound to save energy in this kitchen.

New Kitchen Built to Fit Your Wife

By Gardner Soule

BUILD the cabinets to fit the woman. Build the shelves to fit the supplies. Build the kitchen to fit the family. Starting with these three principles, Cornell University has re-engineered the most-used room in the house.

SERVE CENTER stores china, glasses, silver and linen where they are close to the dining area, located at right above.

RANGE CEN... electric b... their cont... a counter... for the ra... into the ca...

The result is a kitchen equippe...
● Cabinet counter tops that are... able—even after installation—t... woman of any height, or arm...
● Shelves or other provision for... all food and equipment.

Popular Science

September 1953

The standard height of kitchen work surfaces—36 inches (91 cm)—is based on the dimensions of the average woman. (Julia Child, at 6 feet, 2 inches, required hers to be 39 inches high.) Although the long-standing practice of shaping the kitchen around the measure of women might seem to be an insidious means of perpetuating gender stereotypes, the designers and government agencies behind this application of anthropometry have typically been motivated by practical, even progressive aims. This magazine article describes a test kitchen developed in 1952 at Cornell University's Housing Research Center with assistance from the United States Department of Agriculture. Like earlier test kitchens, its design was based on time-motion studies and intended to alleviate the burden of labor.

MIX CENTER contains built-in bins for flour and sugar and a flour sifter. There's an electric outlet for the mixer. Cake pans are racked in cabinet below the counter.

OVEN AND REFRIGERATOR are both waist-high at center for greater accessibility. Refrigerator contains freeze chest and pull-out drawers that eliminate reaching in.

as storage bins r fruits, vegeta- rgents. There's l chair so the sit at the sink. y be added.

e work center tailored to fit y now, and ready to be taken time by a handy man for re- nt to meet new family needs. e things, and many other fresh e included in the kitchen be-

cause so many experts worked on it. The experts came from the campus, from manufacturers, from federal, state and private agencies. Their work was coordinated by Glenn H. Beyer, professor of Housing and Design, and director of

12–Cut
Pie Marker

1950s

UNKNOWN DESIGNER.
12-CUT PIE MARKER. 1950s

Cast aluminum, 2 ½ x 9 ⅝"
diam. (6.4 x 24.4 cm)
Manufactured in Italy.
Department Purchase, 1956

"When, in 1938, the personal desire for coffee came up, my aspect simply was: a coffeemaker must make coffee, and then I applied my knowledge of physics and chemistry," Schlumbohm said. Inspired in spirit by the Bauhaus school of design and in form by laboratory equipment such as the Erlenmeyer flask, the Chemex Coffee Maker is Schlumbohm's most successful design (in 1957 it appeared on James Bond's breakfast table in Ian Fleming's novel *From Russia with Love*). It is part of a unified series of affordable, nonelectrical, nonmechanical kitchenware he designed from the 1940s to the 1960s—including cocktail shakers, ice vaults, kettles, jugs, bottle coolers, and other coffee and tea makers. They epitomize the kitchen-as-laboratory concept (a hallmark of the interwar New Kitchen) as it continued beyond World War II. Over his dynamic career, Schlumbohm obtained over three hundred patents.

Chemex Coffee Maker

1941

PETER SCHLUMBOHM
(AMERICAN, BORN GERMANY. 1896-1962). COFFEE MAKER. 1941

Borosilicate glass (Pyrex), wood, and leather, 9 ½ x 6 ⅛" diam. (24.2 x 15.5 cm). Manufactured by Chemex Corp., New York. Gift of Lewis & Conger, 1943

Chemex Tea Maker

1954

PETER SCHLUMBOHM
(AMERICAN, BORN GERMANY. 1896-1962). TEA MAKER. 1954

Borosilicate glass (Pyrex), wood, steel, and plastic, 7 x 7 ⅜" diam. (17.8 x 18.7 cm). Manufactured by Chemex Corp., New York. Gift of the manufacturer, 1956

Chemex Water Kettle

1949

PETER SCHLUMBOHM
(AMERICAN, BORN
GERMANY. 1896-1962).
WATER KETTLE. 1949

Borosilicate glass (Pyrex)
and cork, kettle: 10 ⅛ x
8 ½" diam. (25.7 x 21.6 cm),
stopper: 6 ¼" (15.9 cm) long.
Manufactured by Chemex
Corp., New York. Gift of
the manufacturer, 1956

Chemex Cocktail Shaker

1943

PETER SCHLUMBOHM
(AMERICAN, BORN GERMANY.
1896-1962). COCKTAIL
SHAKER. 1943

Aluminum, cork, and wood,
shaker: 9 ½ x 4" diam. (24.1 x
10.2 cm), stopper: 3 x 3 ¾"
diam. (7.6 x 9.5 cm), mixer:
12 ¼ x 3" diam. (31.1 x 7.6 cm).
Manufactured by Chemex
Corp., New York. Gift of the
manufacturer, 1956

Exhibition House Kitchen

1950

In 1950, visitors to The Museum of Modern Art could explore Ain's compact three-bedroom Exhibition House (co-sponsored by *Woman's Home Companion* magazine) in the sculpture garden. It was outfitted with modern furniture, lighting, and houseware (including Revere Ware and Ekco tools in the kitchen), representing the design standards the Museum promoted in the same period in its influential exhibition series Useful Objects (1938–48) and Good Design (1950–55). This view includes the Health Chair (foreground), designed in 1938–40 by the Ironrite Ironer Company in Detroit for use with the electric ironing machines it had manufactured since 1911. Ensuring a "scientifically correct ironing posture," this chair exemplifies the application of ergonomics to the banishment of drudgery from the modern kitchen.

INSTALLATION VIEW OF THE KITCHEN IN THE EXHIBITION HOUSE BY **GREGORY AIN,** MAY 17– OCTOBER 29, 1950. THE MUSEUM OF MODERN ART, NEW YORK

Gelatin silver print, 7 ½ x 9 ½" (19 x 24.1 cm). The Museum of Modern Art Archives, New York

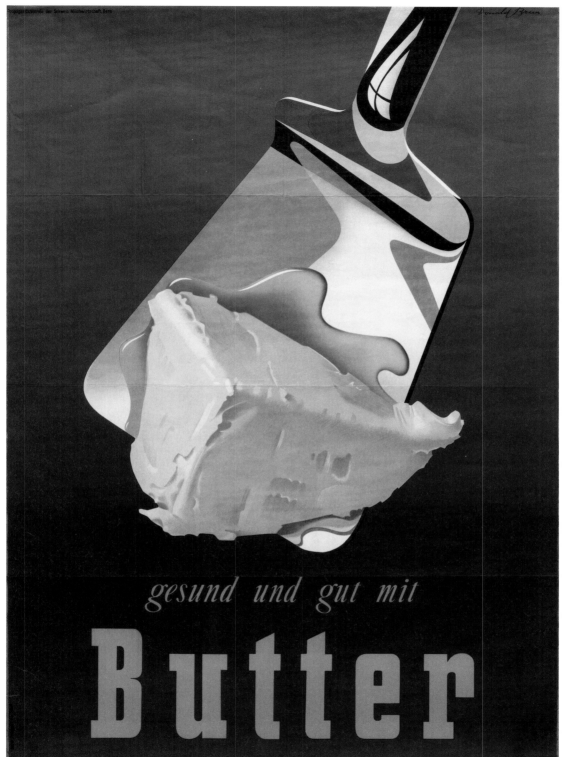

gesund und gut mit

Butter

Healthy and Good with Butter

1951

DONALD BRUN (SWISS, 1909–1999). *GESUND UND GUT MIT BUTTER* (HEALTHY AND GOOD WITH BUTTER). 1951

Offset lithograph, 49 3/4 x 35" (126.4 x 88.8 cm). Printed by Frobenius AG, Basel. Purchase and partial gift of Leslie J. Schrayer, 1994

Tupperware Party, Sarasota, Florida

1958

In 1947 Earl Tupper, an inventor and chemist at DuPont, designed a unique air- and watertight seal for food containers that prevented both spills and spoilage. He then applied this enhancement, the Tupper Seal, to his range of polyethylene Welcome Ware, developed years earlier. The result—Tupperware—became a powerful symbol of suburban domestic life in the 1950s. In addition to its cutting-edge material and form, Tupperware's innovative marketing secured its success. Brownie Wise, a single mother who ultimately became vice president of the company, devised the hostess-party model, in which housewives sold Tupperware to earn money independently (as she demonstrates in this photograph by Steinmetz).

JOE STEINMETZ
(AMERICAN, 1905–1985).
*TUPPERWARE PARTY,
SARASOTA, FLORIDA.* 1958

Gelatin silver print, 10 1/16 x
12 15/16" (25.5 x 32.9 cm). Gift
of Barbara Norfleet, 1984

As Tupperware grew in popularity in the United States, the Milan-based plastics manufacturer Kartell was establishing itself as a European leader in the increasingly important modern material. Colombini, who headed Kartell's technical department from its founding in 1949, was awarded Compasso d'Oro prizes (Italy's top honor for good design) in 1955, 1957, 1959, and 1960. His household objects, including those for the kitchen, took advantage of the aesthetic possibilities of plastic in addition to being both economical and durable.

GINO COLOMBINI
(ITALIAN, BORN 1915).
KITCHEN PAIL. 1957

Polyethylene, 10 ½ x 11"
diam. (26.7 x 27.9 cm).
Manufactured by Kartell
SpA, Milan. Gift of
the manufacturer, 1958

Kitchen Pail

1957

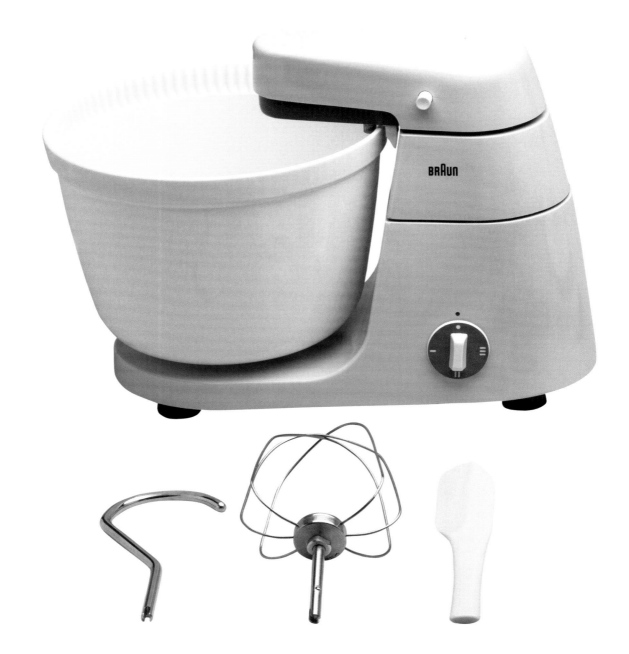

Braun Multipurpose Kitchen Machine

1957

Braun was founded in Frankfurt in 1921 as a small engineering shop producing radio accessories. Dieter Rams, the famous design director who joined the company in 1955 and remained for almost thirty years, secured Braun's success in the postwar consumer electronics market. The company's radios, scales, fans, mixers, slide projectors, calculators, hair dryers, toasters, and juicers, as well as this Multipurpose Kitchen Machine, all embody Rams's mission to "omit the unimportant," and they fulfill this directive by founder Max Braun's son, Erwin: "Our electrical appliances should be quiet, unobtrusive helpers and servants. Like a good servant in days of old, they should come and go silently, there when wanted but unnoticed."

BRAUN AG (GERMANY,
EST. 1921). MULTIPURPOSE
KITCHEN MACHINE. 1957

Enameled metal casing and
plastic, blender configuration:
19 ¼ x 13 x 6 ½" (48.9 x 33
x 16.5 cm). Manufactured
by Braun AG, Frankfurt.
Gift of the manufacturer

Sarpaneva's cast iron casserole has become an iconic work of organic design. It is one of several objects that represent his interest in kitchenware that could be used in the oven, on the stovetop, and at the table (sometimes also in the refrigerator). The teak handle allows it to be carried by one hand, and when removed it can be used to open the pot's lid. Along with contemporaries such as Kaj Franck and Tapio Wirkkala, Sarpaneva achieved international fame as the clean and warm modern forms of Finnish design grew in popularity in the postwar period.

TIMO SARPANEVA
(FINNISH, 1926–2006).
CASSEROLE. 1959

Cast iron and teak, overall:
7 x 8 x 7¾" (17.8 x 20.3 x 19.7 cm). Manufactured by W. Rosenlew and Co., Finland. Gift of the designer, 1990

Casserole

1959

PETER RAACKE (GERMAN, BORN 1928). MONO 10+1 KITCHEN TOOL SET. 1965

Stainless steel, length of bar rack: 9¼" (23.5 cm), skimmer: 13½" (34.3 cm), spatula: 13⅝" (34.6 cm), knife: 11⁵⁄₁₆" (28.7 cm), perforated spoon: 10³⁄₁₆" (22.9 cm), spoon: 10³⁄₁₆" (25.9 cm), ladle: 9" (34.6 cm), small two-pronged fork: 13¾" (34.9 cm), small ladle: 10⅛" (25.7 cm), two-pronged fork: 10¾" (27.3 cm). Manufactured by Hessische Metallwerke (now Seibel Designpartner GmbH), Germany. Gift of Bonniers, Inc., 1967

mono 10+1
Kitchen Tool Set

1965

This set of kitchen utensils belongs to the clean-lined, stainless steel "mono" series for which Raacke is best known. It debuted in the late 1950s with mono-a, which was followed by numerous iterations into the early 1980s, including mono petit, for children. Raacke, who trained in gold- and silversmithing, also designed cardboard furniture and a diesel locomotive. He cofounded the Association of German Industrial Designers in 1959 and taught for more than thirty years at major German universities. Along with Max Bill, he is associated with the reemergence of so-called Good Design in Europe after World War II.

SOVIET PREMIER NIKITA
KHRUSHCHEV AND
UNITED STATES VICE
PRESIDENT RICHARD
NIXON AT THE AMERICAN
NATIONAL EXHIBITION,
MOSCOW, JULY 1959

The Kitchen Debate

July 1959

"I want to show you this kitchen," said Richard Nixon. "It's like those of houses in California . . . " So began the famous Cold War confrontation known as the Kitchen Debate, between Nixon, then vice president of the United States, and Soviet premier Nikita Khrushchev in the General Electric kitchen at the opening of the American National Exhibition in Moscow. Nixon fixed on the familiar and symbolic setting of the kitchen to extol American abundance, innovation, freedom of choice, and quality of life—and, by extension, capitalism itself. "Would it not be better," he challenged Khrushchev, "to compete in the relative merit of washing machines than in the strength of rockets?" "And this is one of the greatest nations?" countered Khrushchev. "I feel sorry for Americans, judging by your exhibition. Does your life really consist only of kitchens?" Such criticism proved ineffectual, however, against the seductive appeal of the American kitchenware that was promoted internationally in the 1950s in traveling exhibitions supported by the State Department, corporations such as General Electric, and The Museum of Modern Art.

This hinged, mobile kitchen on castors incorporates a stove, a small refrigerator, a pull-out cutting board, and a surprising abundance of storage space. It was shown in The Museum of Modern Art's landmark 1972 exhibition *Italy: The New Domestic Landscape*, which celebrated innovative, flexible designs responsive to new ideas about casual and adaptable living. In considering this dynamic, compact unit, *Time* magazine noted its cultural significance: "In a country like Italy, where the kitchen is still a kind of sacred cave presided over by a mother-goddess, the design of a cooking module that can be rolled about and plugged in anywhere has profound implications. Not, perhaps, the immediate death of the nuclear family—but certainly a substantive critique of it."

VIRGILIO FORCHIASSIN (ITALIAN). SPAZIO VIVO (LIVING SPACE) MOBILE KITCHEN UNIT. 1968

Steel and plywood covered with plastic laminate, closed: 36 ¼ x 48 ⅞ x 48 ⅞" (92 x 124 x 124 cm). Manufactured by Snaidero, Italy. Gift of the manufacturer, 1972

Living Space Mobile Kitchen Unit

1968

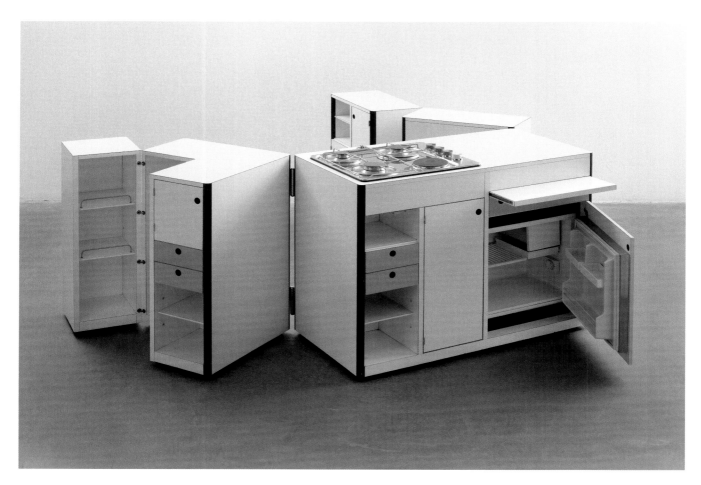

Kitchen
Scale
1969

MARCO ZANUSO
(ITALIAN, 1916–2001).
KITCHEN SCALE
(MODEL BA 2000). 1969

ABS polymer casing,
6 ⅛ x 6 ½ x 4 ⅛" (15.5 x 16.5
x 10.5 cm). Manufactured
by Terraillon SLR, Italy. Gift
of the manufacturer, 1970

TOP RIGHT:

TOM WESSELMANN
(AMERICAN, 1931-2004).
STILL LIFE #30. APRIL 1963

Oil, enamel, and synthetic
polymer paint on composition
board with collage of printed
advertisements, plastic
flowers, refrigerator door,
plastic replicas of 7-Up
bottles, glazed and framed
color reproduction, and
stamped metal, 48 ½ x 66 x 4"
(122 x 167.5 x 10 cm). Gift of
Philip Johnson, 1970

BELOW, LEFT:

ANDY WARHOL
(AMERICAN, 1928-1987).
BRILLO BOX (SOAP PADS).
1964

Synthetic polymer paint
and silkscreen ink on wood,
each: 17 ⅛ x 17 x 14"
(43.3 x 43.2 x 36.5 cm).
Gifts of Doris and Donald
Fisher, 1997

CENTER:

ANDY WARHOL
(AMERICAN, 1928-1987).
*HEINZ TOMATO KETCHUP
BOX [PROTOTYPE].* 1963-64

Synthetic polymer paint
and silkscreen ink on
wood, 10 ½ x 15 ½ x 10 ½"
(26.7 x 39.4 x 26.7 cm).
Gift of Jasper Johns, 1998

RIGHT:

ANDY WARHOL
(AMERICAN, 1928-1987).
*CAMPBELL'S TOMATO JUICE
BOX.* 1964

Synthetic polymer paint
and silkscreen ink on wood,
10 x 19 x 9 ½" (25.4 x 48.3 x
24.1 cm). Gift of Douglas
S. Cramer Foundation, 1997

View of Counter Space: Design and the Modern Kitchen, The Museum of Modern Art, New York

September 15, 2010–
May 2, 2011

Delphic
Kitchen Utility
Blades

1973

HARRY V. CREMONESE
(AMERICAN, BORN ANTHONY
C. CANNON 1939). DELPHIC
KITCHEN UTILITY BLADES. 1973

Carbon stainless steel and
beechwood, left to right: 15 x
3 3/8 x 3/4" (38.1 x 8.6 x 1.9 cm),
13 x 2 3/4 x 3/4" (33 x 7 x 1.9 cm),
11 x 2 1/2 x 1/2" (27.9 x 6.4 x 1.3
cm). Manufactured by Mitsuboshi
Company, Seki-city, Gifu, Japan.
Gift of the designer, 1977

Good
Grips
Peeler

1989

SMART DESIGN
(USA, EST. 1979). GOOD
GRIPS PEELER. 1989

Stainless steel and synthetic
rubber, 8 3/4 x 1 3/8 x 1" (22.2 x
12.7 x 2.5 cm). Manufactured
by OXO International, New York.
Gift of the designers, 1994

Ergonomi Kitchen Knife and Cutting Board

1973

ERGONOMI DESIGN GRUPPEN (SWEDEN, EST. 1969). MARIA BENKTZON (SWEDISH, BORN 1946). SVEN-ERIC JUHLIN (SWEDISH, BORN 1940). KITCHEN KNIFE AND CUTTING BOARD. 1973

Knife: stainless steel and polypropylene, 13 ½ x 4 x 1" (34.3 cm x 10.2 x 2.5 cm), cutting board: plastic, 5 ¼ x 15 ¹⁄₁₆ x 5 ³⁄₈" (13.3 x 38.3 x 13.7 cm). Manufactured by AB Gustavsberg, Sweden. Gift of RFSU Rehab, 1983

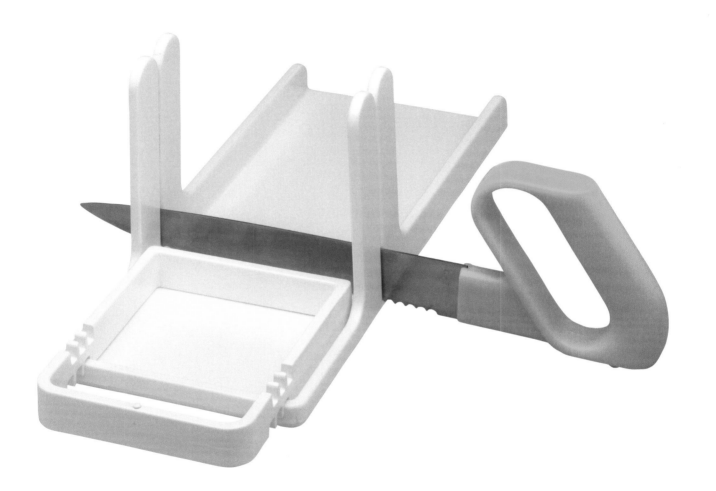

While designers often reimagine the standard forms of kitchen tools for aesthetic reasons or to utilize new materials, this work incorporates ergonomic changes intended to make familiar objects more accessible. It was featured in The Museum of Modern Art's 1988 exhibition *Design for Independent Living*, which highlighted the efforts of designers to meet the needs of the elderly and people with physical disabilities. Ergoncmi Design has specialized in this area since 1969, reflecting through its award-winning products and its motto—"Innovation for People"—an outstanding commitment to diverse user needs. The company's work from the 1970s and 1980s, much of which is still in production today, represents the progressive "democratic" design that has long been associated with the historically equality-driven culture of Sweden.

Alcan Foil
in the Kitchen

ALCAN FOIL

Alcan Foil
for Cooking

ALCAN FOIL

Alcan Foil
Brochures

c. 1960-62

ROLF HARDER
(GERMAN, BORN 1929).
ALCAN FOIL BROCHURES
FOR THE ALUMINUM
COMPANY OF CANADA.
c. 1960-62

Offset lithographs, each:
8 x 4" (20.3 x 10.2 cm).
Gifts of the designer, 2007

"Most metals," explained *Popular Science* magazine in 1936, "are as old as history. Lead was used by the ancient Romans. Iron and copper go back to 3,000 years before the birth of Christ. But aluminum, in contrast, is a modern metal of the laboratory." Although it is the most common metal in the earth's crust, aluminum was too difficult to isolate and too expensive for commercial use until the turn of the twentieth century. Industrial rolling of aluminum foil had begun by 1910 in Switzerland, and in the 1950s, after the metal rationing of World War II, production and consumption of aluminum foil exploded. Like plastic, aluminum is a modern material that has revolutionized both industry and daily life (from aerospace design to microwave dinners), and aluminum foil has become an indispensible tool of the modern kitchen. The strength, malleability, heat conductivity, recyclability, resistance to corrosion, and barrier properties of the aluminum alloy sheet translate to countless applications in cooking and storage as well as commercial food packaging. These brochures illustrate various uses for the foil produced by the Aluminum Company of Canada.

"One-third of a worker's salary is spent for fuel . . . while from eight to nine months a year the sun shines all day," Tarcici said in Lebanon in 1955. Beginning in the 1950s, the professor and United Nations delegate achieved numerous patents for solar cooker designs, including this one, which collapses completely into the portable box that also serves as its spine. Attempts to harness the sun's power for cooking had been made in the late nineteenth century; the Association for Applied Solar Energy (later the International Solar Energy Society) was formed in 1955. In 1956 a *New York Times* article featured Tarcici, who was pictured cooking hot dogs with one of his own devices.

Solnar Solar Cooker

c. 1970

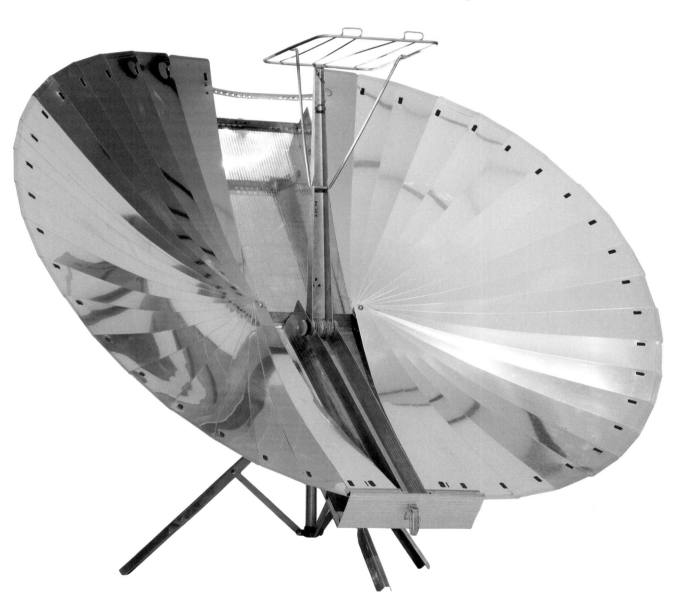

ADNAN TARCICI (YEMENI, BORN LEBANON 1918). SOLNAR SOLAR COOKER. c. 1970

Aluminum, open: 21 x 34 x 43" (53.3 x 86.3 x 109.2 cm), closed: 8 ½ x 2 ¾" (21.6 x 7 cm). Gift of the designer, 1974

Japanese Plastic Food

c. 1975

In Japan, *shokuhin sanpuru*—plastic food designed and manufactured for restaurant display—is a major national industry. Models of Japanese and Western foods are molded and painted in exquisite detail to look as good as their edible counterparts, if not better. Displayed in a restaurant's front window, these durable replicas facilitate interlingual communication and allow customers to identify food names and prices. The Japanese practice of creating replica food (in wax, before plastic) dates back to around 1920 and was reportedly inspired by the lifelike anatomical teaching models then being imported from the United States by new medical schools. The industry boomed after 1960, when restaurants began offering more varied menus. The realistic models are also commonly used as stand-ins for commercials and are sold to tourists as souvenirs.

UNKNOWN DESIGNER.
JAPANESE PLASTIC FOOD.
c. 1975

Plastic, hamburger: 3 ½ x 4"
diam. (8.9 x 10.2 cm).
Manufactured in Kappabashi,
Tokyo. Greta Daniel Fund and
Yale University Fund, 1977.
Installation view of *Counter
Space: Design and the Modern
Kitchen*, The Museum of Modern
Art, New York, September 15,
2010–May 2, 2011

Juicy Salif
Lemon
Squeezer

1988

PHILIPPE STARCK
(FRENCH, BORN 1949).
JUICY SALIF LEMON
SQUEEZER. 1988

Polytetrafluoroethylene
(PTFE) treated pressure-cast
aluminum and polyamide,
11 ½ x 5" (29.2 x 12.7 cm).
Manufactured by Officina
Alessi, Italy. David Whitney
Collection. Gift of David
Whitney, 2000

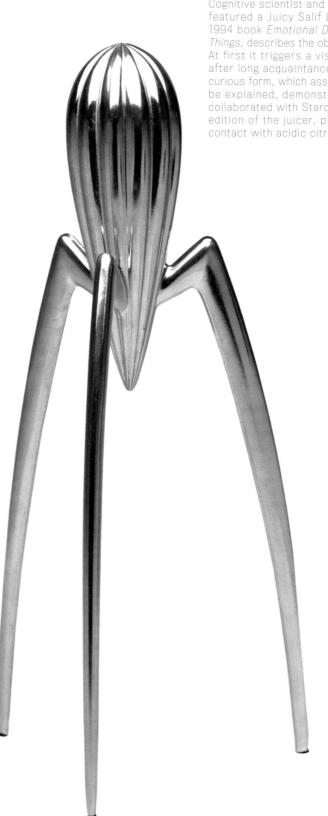

"My juicer is not meant to squeeze lemons; it is meant to start conversations," Starck has reportedly said of this object. Cognitive scientist and design consultant Donald Norman, who featured a Juicy Salif Lemon Squeezer on the cover of his 1994 book *Emotional Design: Why We Love (or Hate) Everyday Things*, describes the object as seductive rather than utilitarian. At first it triggers a visceral reaction, he explains, and even after long acquaintance it maintains "reflective" appeal; the curious form, which associates a routine task with glamour, must be explained, demonstrated, shown off. Alessi, which has collaborated with Starck since 1986, produced an anniversary edition of the juicer, plated in gold, with instruction against contact with acidic citrus fruits.

**Judy Holliday in
Full of Life**

1956

RICHARD QUINE
(AMERICAN, 1920–1989).
FULL OF LIFE. 1956. USA

35mm film (black and white,
sound). 91 min.

Kitchen Sink Dramas

4
—

In lived experience, the modern kitchen is often a far cry from the visions of architects, designers, manufacturers, and advertisers. It is a place of mess and mishap, socialization and sensuality. It evokes a gamut of emotions, fostering creativity and genuine pleasure as well as anxiety—manifested in the extreme as mageirocophobia, the fear of cooking. It is also, statistics confirm, the most dangerous room in the home.

As spaces we occupy and animate daily and that are constantly reflected back to us in popular media, kitchens have since the 1960s become an increasingly rich subject for artistic expression. For Pop artists, the proliferation of branded goods in the kitchen provided a powerful visual currency, but such visions of plenty were not embraced by all. Artists, activists, and designers began to critique the modern kitchen as emblematic of much that was wrong with modern society, representative of unsustainable levels of waste and imposed social conformity. They questioned modernism's disregard for social inequality and cultural difference in promoting universal ideals. Feminists condemned designs, including the Frankfurt Kitchen, that they felt reinforced the physical and psychological isolation of women in the home. They exposed mythologies that disguised and devalued women's domestic work with veils of "labor-saving" and "leisure."

The term "kitchen sink drama" refers to the postwar British cultural movement in which artists brought into focus the everyday experiences of alienated working-class characters. However, as the varied works in this section demonstrate, the familiar setting of the kitchen is employed by all kinds of artists, taking divergent forms and critical positions. Here kitchens are addressed as dreams, nightmares, and battlegrounds, challenging us to consider larger issues surrounding popular culture, consumerism, gender, and the intimate realities of domestic life.

The cost of bringing the Absolute into the kitchen is to soil it. The pretensions of Good Design require us to bring the noblest concepts of the humanistic tradition into direct confrontation with scrambled egg and soiled nappies. . . . The big white abstractions must be devalued, ultimately, by these associations with dirt and muck and domestic grottitude.

REYNER BANHAM, "HOUSEHOLD GODJETS," 1970

DANIEL SPOERRI
(SWISS, BORN ROMANIA
1930). *KICHKA'S
BREAKFAST I*. 1960

Wood chair hung on wall
with board across seat,
coffeepot, tumbler, china,
eggcups, eggshells, cigarette
butts, spoons, tin cans,
etc., 14 $^3/_8$ x 27 $^3/_8$ x 25 $^3/_4$"
(36.6 x 69.5 x 65.4 cm).
Philip Johnson Fund, 1961

Kichka's Breakfast I

1960

Spoerri, a self-proclaimed "paster of found situations," made
this assemblage from his girlfriend Kichka's leftovers while
waiting for some visitors. "I pasted together the morning's
breakfast, which was still there by chance," he has explained.
Comprising dishes, utensils, food, cigarettes, and a small chair
and wood panel, the work is displayed on the wall, where it
"defies the laws of gravity" and "the view to which we are
accustomed," the artist has said.

Dropped
Cup of Coffee

1967

CLAES OLDENBURG
(AMERICAN, BORN SWEDEN
1929). *DROPPED CUP OF
COFFEE: PRELIMINARY
STUDY FOR "IMAGE OF THE
BUDDHA PREACHING"
BY FRANK O'HARA.* 1967

Pencil, crayon, and wash on
paper, 30 ⅛ x 22 ⅛" (76.5 x 56.4
cm). Gift of the artist, 1967

Untitled

c. 1972

WILLIAM EGGLESTON
(AMERICAN, BORN 1939).
UNTITLED FROM THE
PORTFOLIO *TROUBLED
WATERS*. c. 1972

Dye transfer print, 11 ½ x
17 ⅜" (29.4 x 44.3 cm).
Gift of Caldecot Chubb,
1986

Memphis

c. 1972

Untitled

Summer 1964

WILLIAM GEDNEY
(AMERICAN, 1932–1989).
UNTITLED. SUMMER 1964

Gelatin silver print, 12 x 8 ¼"
(30.5 x 20.9 cm). Mr. and Mrs.
John Spencer Fund, 1969

Kitchen,
Kensington,
California

1968

CHAUNCEY HARE
(AMERICAN, BORN 1934).
*KITCHEN, KENSINGTON,
CALIFORNIA.* 1968

Gelatin silver print,
8 ½ x 12" (21.6 x 30.5 cm).
Purchase, 1969

Untitled
Film Still #84

1980

CINDY SHERMAN
(AMERICAN, BORN 1954).
*UNTITLED FILM STILL
#84*. 1980

Gelatin silver print,
7 ½ x 9 ⁷⁄₁₆" (19.1 x 24 cm).
Purchase, 1995

Blonde/
Red Dress/
Kitchen

1978

LAURIE SIMMONS
(AMERICAN, BORN 1949).
*BLONDE/RED DRESS/
KITCHEN* FROM THE SERIES
INTERIORS. 1978

Silver dye bleach print,
3 ¼ x 5" (8.3 x 12.7 cm).
Joel and Anne Ehrenkranz
Fund, 1994

Since the mid-1970s Simmons has constructed and photographed dollhouse scenes that reflect on and critique the culture of domesticity. "Setting up small rooms with dolls in them was a way for me to experience photography without taking my camera out to the street," she has said of this work. ". . . The chairs, the food, the stove, the sink, the woman. I like the way they all occupy the same importance in the picture. I like the way, in that kitchen, it's always five after six. It's always the dinner hour. I see these pictures as being a little lonely, like where is the rest of the world, where are the other people, where's the rest of the family? . . . It's interesting for me that a picture can be so colorful and so bright and so vivacious and so lonely at the same time."

To Make
Meringue . . .

1998

DAVID SHRIGLEY (BRITISH,
BORN 1968). *TO MAKE
MERINGUE YOU MUST BEAT
THE EGG WHITES UNTIL THEY
LOOK LIKE THIS*. 1998

Artist's book, cover: 9 ⁷⁄₁₆ x
8 ⅛" (24 x 20.7 cm). Publisher:
Galleri Nicolai Wallner,
Copenhagen. Edition: 2,000.
Anonymous gift, 2002

Untitled

1984–87

MARY E. FREY
(AMERICAN, BORN 1948).
UNTITLED FROM THE SERIES
REAL LIFE DRAMAS. 1984–87

Chromogenic color print, 24 x
20" (61 x 50.8 cm). Gift of the
photographer, 1987

"But how can you be certain?" she asked.
"You never can," was her reply.

Fork in Refrigerator

1975

JAMES CASEBERE
(AMERICAN, BORN 1953).
FORK IN REFRIGERATOR.
1975

Gelatin silver print,
9 3/8 x 6 5/16" (23.8 x 16 cm).
Fractional and promised gift
of David Teiger, 2006

The
Toaster

1976

MAC ADAMS
(AMERICAN, BORN 1943).
THE TOASTER. 1976

Gelatin silver prints,
each: 28 ³⁄₄ x 32 ⁷⁄₈"
(73 x 83.5 cm). Gift of
the photographer, 1992

Untitled

1980

JAMES ROSENQUIST
(AMERICAN, BORN 1933).
UNTITLED. 1980

Oil on canvas, 6' 6 ⅛" x 66"
(198.4 x 167.6 cm). Gift of
Philip Johnson, 1998

PHILIP-LORCA DICORCIA
(AMERICAN, BORN 1953).
AUDEN. 1988

Chromogenic color print,
15 ⅜ x 22 ⁷⁄₁₆" (39 x 57 cm).
Gift of Carol and Arthur
Goldberg, 2001

ANNA BLUME (GERMAN,
BORN 1937). **BERNHARD
BLUME** (GERMAN,
BORN 1937). *KITCHEN
FRENZY*. 1986

Gelatin silver prints,
each: 66 ¹⁵⁄₁₆ x 42 ½" (170 x
108 cm). Acquired through
the generosity of the
Contemporary Arts Council
of The Museum of Modern
Art, 1989

Kitchen Frenzy, starring Anna Blume in the guise of a stereo-typical housewife, is marked by an ironic sense of humor that is part surreal and part burlesque. The sequence shows a domestic interior run amok, with potatoes flying of their own volition at all angles. The title, a pun on the condition known as "prison frenzy"—the insanity that sets in when inmates are imprisoned for long periods of time—wryly plays with the daily rituals of traditional suburban life. The absurd and humorous quality of the Blumes' work stems largely from their original staging of scenarios that, rendered with the blur of motion, slyly undermine certainties about human reason and social order.

Kitchen Frenzy

1986

Jack Lemmon and Shirley MacLaine in The Apartment

1960

BILLY WILDER (AMERICAN, BORN AUSTRIA-HUNGARY [NOW POLAND]. 1906-2002). *THE APARTMENT*. 1960. USA

35mm film (black and white, sound). 125 min.

LUCAS SAMARAS
(AMERICAN, BORN GREECE
1936). *ADJUSTMENT.*
JANUARY 19, 1986

Collage of color instant prints
(Polacolor ER), 13 7/8 x 15 7/8"
(35.3 x 40.3 cm). Gift of Robert
and Gayle Greenhil, 1992

Adjustment

January 19, 1986

Harsh lighting, an unstable viewpoint, and macabre, incon-
gruous objects have transformed this kitchen from a center
of domestic comfort to a site of unease, constriction, and
psychological fragmentation. Samaras's work in various mediums
focuses on almost obsessional self-observation. This portrait
picturing the artist in his New York apartment is an unusual
example of a male artist representing himself in his kitchen.

Emptying
the
Fridge

1984

MICHAEL MANDEL
(AMERICAN, BORN 1950).
EMPTYING THE FRIDGE.
1984

Silver dye bleach print,
15 ⁷⁄₈ x 19 ⁷⁄₈" (40.6 x 50.7 cm).
The Family of Man Fund, 1985

Untitled

2005

With its door shut, in many homes the bulky form of the refriger-ator and its bountiful contents recede from view, appearing to merge seamlessly with the overall impression of a modern fitted kitchen. Shrigley highlights the way in which the complex mechanical workings of most appliances are now disguised by design that emphasizes their symbolic rather than practical role in modern life. On another level, the white rectangle wittily updates Kazimir Malevich's iconic *Black Square* painting of 1913 as a statement of existential "nothingness" in twenty-first-century culture.

DAVID SHRIGLEY (BRITISH, BORN 1968). *UNTITLED*. 2005

One from an untitled portfolio of twenty-two woodcuts, sheet: 23 9/16 x 15 11/16" (59.8 x 39.9 cm). Publisher: Galleri Nicolai Wallner, Copenhagen. Printer: Schaefer Grafiske Vaerksted, Copenhagen. Edition: 20. The Associates Fund, 2006

Colophon

Published in conjunction with the exhibition *Counter Space: Design and the Modern Kitchen*, organized by Juliet Kinchin, Curator, and Aidan O'Connor, Curatorial Assistant, Department of Architecture and Design, September 15, 2010–May 2, 2011. For further reading and resources, please visit the exhibition's Web site, at MoMA.org/counterspace.

The exhibition is supported by Silestone Quartz Surfaces.

This publication was made possible by the Nancy Lee and Perry Bass Publication Endowment Fund.

Produced by the Department of Publications, The Museum of Modern Art, New York

Edited by Rebecca Roberts
Designed by Triboro
Production by Marc Sapir with Tiffany Hu

Printed and bound by CS Graphics Pte Ltd., Singapore

This book was typeset in Brauer Neue and Titling Gothic. The paper is 135 gsm Gardapat Kiara.

Published by The Museum of Modern Art
11 West 53 Street
New York, New York
10019-5497
www.moma.org

Library of Congress Control Number: 2010942821

ISBN: 978-0-87070-808-4

Distributed in the United States and Canada by D.A.P/ Distributed Art Publishers, Inc., 155 Sixth Avenue, 2nd floor New York, New York 10013
www.artbook.com

Distributed outside the United States and Canada by Thames & Hudson Ltd., 181 High Holborn, London WC1V 7QX
www.thamesandhudson.com

Printed in Singapore

Photograph Credits

Acknowledgments

As one of the Museum's security guards aptly observed on opening day, *Counter Space: Design and the Modern Kitchen* is a big exhibition in a small gallery. We are so grateful to the very many people who helped us realize our ambitious plans.

For vital support we wish first to thank Glenn D. Lowry, director of The Museum of Modern Art, and the Museum's board of trustees. We also thank the exhibition's supporter, Silestone Quartz Surfaces.

We are grateful to the leaders of the various teams at the Museum that helped make *Counter Space* happen, especially Ramona Bannayan, Deputy Director for Exhibitions and Collections; Maria DeMarco Beardsley, Coordinator of Exhibitions; Jerry Neuner, Director, Department of Exhibition Design and Production; Julia Hoffmann, Creative Director of Advertising and Graphic Design; Wendy Woon, Deputy Director for Education; and Rob Jung, Manager, and Sarah Wood, Assistant Manager, Art Handling and Preparation.

From our core exhibition team we thank, in particular, Lana Hum, Production Manager, Department of Exhibition Design and Production, whose positive spirit and tireless dedication created a beautiful installation design from our sometimes kooky ideas; Randolph Black, Associate Coordinator of Exhibitions, who was a keen and gracious exhibition manager; and Steven Wheeler, Assistant Registrar, who provided razor-sharp registrarial oversight with great patience. Special thanks are extended also to our delightful intern Juliana Barton, who tackled even wearisome projects with enthusiasm and professionalism.

In the Department of Architecture and Design we are grateful for the support of Barry Bergdoll, Chief Curator, and the entire staff. We give special thanks to Paul Galloway, Study Center Supervisor; Whitney May, Department Assistant; Pamela Popeson, Preparator; Emma Presler, Department Manager; and Margot Weller, Curatorial Assistant.

Counter Space would have been a much narrower exhibition without assistance from the Museum's other curatorial departments. We are grateful to our generous colleagues who facilitated crucial internal loans: Kathy Curry, Department of Drawings; Rajendra Roy and Katie Trainor, Department of Film; Barbara London and Katelyn Nomura-Weingrow, Department of Media and Performance Art; Cora Rosevear, Department of Painting and Sculpture; Dan Leers and Eva Respini, Department of Photography; and Gretchen Wagner, Department of Prints and Illustrated Books. And, as always, we are indebted to the expert team in the Department of Conservation, including Roger Griffith, Margo Delidow, Lynda Zycherman, Karl Buchberg, Erika Mosier, Scott Gerson, and intern Christian Imhoff.

The creation of this book was a thrilling bonus, conceived after the exhibition opened. It was edited by the incomparable Rebecca Roberts, Senior Assistant Editor, Department of Publications, and designed by Stefanie Weigler and David Heasty of Triboro. We sincerely thank the Department of Publications for the opportunity to do this project, especially our magnanimous managers, Marc Sapir, Production Director, and Kara Kirk, Associate Publisher.

We also wish to recognize the contributions of the following people inside and outside the Museum, with thanks: Nancy Adelson, Michael Alfano, Michele Arms, Karlyn Benson, Sara Bodinson, Anthony Bonino, Sean Brown, Tomasz Choros, Claire Corey, Inva Cota, Margaret Doyle, D'Arcy Drollinger, Jason Fry, Libby Hruska, Tiffany Hu, Milan Hughston, Anthony Jones, Charlie Kalinowski, Robert Kastler, Tom Krueger, Erik Landsberg, Rosa Laster-Smith, Kim Loewe, Nathaniel Longcope, Maria Marchenkova, Jonathan Muzikar, Stephanie Pau, Bryan Reyna, Roberto Rivera, David Senior, Allan Smith, Heidi Spekhart, Lauren Stakias, Jennifer Tobias, John Tolentino, Harvey Tulcensky, Yanik Wagner, Mark Warhall, Steve West, Jeff White, Mark Williams, Adam Wojtyna, and John Wood.

We extend a special "cheers" to our colleagues who went above and beyond for *Counter Space*: Brigitta Bungard, Graphic Design Manager; Elizabeth Riggle, Preparator; Howard Deitch, Mike Gibbons, and Lucas Gonzalez, A/V Technicians; and Peter Perez, Foreman, and his team in the frame shop.

Vielen Dank to Astrid Debus-Steinberg and Martina Debus, our friends and true Frankfurt Kitchen experts.

Finally, thank you to Paul Stirton and *Counter Space*-titler Andrew Ashwood, brilliant partners who make everything tickety-boo.

Juliet Kinchin, Curator, and Aidan O'Connor, Curatorial Assistant
Department of Architecture and Design